The Shaman Speaks

The Shaman Speaks
© Joseph Murphy, 2019

No part of this book may be reproduced by any means known at this time or derived henceforth without written permission of the publisher or author. The exception would be in the case of brief quotations embodied in the critical articles or reviews and pages where permission is specifically granted by the publisher or author.

Books may be purchased in quantity and/or special sales by contacting the publisher. All inquiries related to such matters should be addressed to:

Middle Creek Publishing & Audio
9167 Pueblo Mountain Park Road
Beulah, CO 81023
editor@middlecreekpublishing.com
(719) 369-9050

First Paperback Edition, 2019
ISBN: 978-1-7332163-8-8
Printed in the United States

Cover Image: wwing / AnsonLu, iStock
Design: David Anthony Martin

The Shaman Speaks

Joseph Murphy

Middle Creek Publishing & Audio
Beulah, CO
↑

ALSO BY JOSEPH MURPHY

Shoreline of the Heart
Shanta Arts Publishing, 2019

Having Lived
Kelsay Books, 2018

Crafting Wings
Scars Publications, 2017

For Frances

Table of Contents

The Shaman's Birth	13
The Shaman's Initiation	14
The Shaman Meets With the Man in the Moon	16
The Shaman's Craft	17
The Shaman's Dream	18
The Shaman's Cure	19
The Shaman Comforts the Fledgling's Soul	21
The Shaman's Journey	22
The Shaman Speaks With the Mother of the Sea Beasts	24
The Shaman and the Goddess	26
The Shaman Meets With the First of the Dead	28
The Shaman and the Oracle	30
The Shaman Visits the House of Dust	31
The Shaman Rises From the Waters of Death	34

True shamans live in a world that is alive with what is to rationalist sight unseen, a world pulsing with intelligence.

— Paula Gunn Allen

The Shaman's Birth

My souls gathered on a lily's stalk,
spinning bone and marrow
from sky-tossed nettle; blood from dew
pooled in a stone's shoal.

As eye and ear emerged,
so did the memory
of talon and beak.

I began to kick in a rhythm drummed by my ancestors.

Guardian spirits
carved sun and moon into rib and skull; shook lightning
from their plumage.

As my souls' wings pressed me through,
all knew what I would become.

My first cry stirred a sapling's leaves,
though the seams of my caul
had yet to burst.

Sea-rounded pebbles were placed in my palms
as this first mask burned.

The Shaman's Initiation

The ring was spun down the spirits' road,
a strand of silk
strung from tree to tree.

I lay in a furrow, covered
with petal and stalk: The chanting began.

I grasped the ring's heart as it came down the road.
A spirit leapt up; pressed me
into its luminous shell.

It pierced my navel, lodging a seed
at the base of my spine.

I rose up nine ladders of yet-to-fall rain;
drew a beam-laced feather
from the moon's crest.

My teacher's drum drew me back: the ring
again took the road. A new spirit
seized me in its talons.

We pressed through jagged, bucking vines;
came to a gnarled gate,
swung open by the spirit's shriek.

I fell to the edge of a pool, white-hot stones
churning at my feet.

The spirit thrust the hottest of these
through my skull: the burning
cleansed my dreams.

My teacher's drum drew me back: down
came the ring; a third spirit
tore off my robe.

Cradled naked in its paws, I was raised
to the horizon's outer-most band,
where I found a cap, coat and belt.

A seven-stepped rainbow shimmered
as I donned these gifts. The spirit
wove me a mask
from strands of cloud and soil
swirling in its pelt;
from star-bright ribbons
raising from its horns.

It beat its mane against my tongue: My mouth
filled with light.

I began to shape words as spirits do.

Again, my teacher's drum: I woke
in the limbs of a tree; silk strands
entwined my naked waist; an iron ring
on my finger,
a drum of my own
in hand.

The Shaman Meets With the Man in the Moon

I grasp rungs of light ascending from a lilac's bud.

Passing the eight-sided mountain's peak,
I draw a dreamer's fingers from my drum's skin:
through them,
reach the final rung.

Guided by an ancestor's cipher, I step
through a maze
as others would a stream.

One of my spirits hisses free before The Gate of Bones.

The bolts groan beneath that spirit's bloodied fins:
hinges splinter;
the dark's distorted echo
recedes.

I pass through and perch on a spoke of light.

The Man in the Moon greets me;
offers a silken thread
entwining each soul I am to return
to body and breath.

When I take it in my beak, I awake
in a pine's topmost limbs
knowing the fullness
of my fate.

The Shaman's Craft

I speak of a boat with a beak at its bow.

Its hull an oath churned from my drum's skin;
decks caulked by song
rising from the wreath within a mountain's tongue.

I raise a mast whittled from a root my kin
pressed between my mother's teeth
as the birthing began.

Tonight, I graze the sky's banks
as branches burst from the husk of my keel.

Only a fool would think I lie at your feet
as a flame's bud opens through the stalk of my chest,
seeds fall from my rudder's quill,
and a new moon's tentacles
hone my oars.

Rolling and twisting,
I rise and weave through a conch shell's song:
the smashed bone of my cap
seething and wailing;
my spiked club
jabbing at coiled shards.

To and fro, I rise from a star-chipped stream,
rowing as I beat on the sail of my lungs;
as I scent from a wolf's snout;
fixed in a puma's stare and stance,
searching for the soul
I've been sent to retrieve.

The Shaman's Dream

Lightning bolts struck my oars
as I rowed the seven-colored sky,
seeking a cure.

I sprang from the bow,
vaulted the moon; steadied
on the tree's top-most,
star-whittled branch.

My feet became talons; my scalp
an iron cap.

Wings spread from the cap's well-etched brim; soaring,
I rose amid sea-rounded spirits; plumage
changing shade and shape.

These spirits whispered chants; preened
my crest, vowed to remain
in the skin of my drum.

I vowed to rise when rain fell
from the sheen of their bones; wear the cloud-grey shells
they offered.

When thunder woke me,
my soaked cap scented of pine;
blood caked my hands.

Shadows of wing, talon and beak
had reshaped me.

The Shaman's Cure

As I ascend, snakes that coil my iron cap
begin to pool and gulp
a mare's well-spend blood.

When I near the tree's uppermost limb
smooth-beaked spirits lunge for my throat:
but my mast holds;
sails taut through pitch and pull,
a shoulder bone my keel.

Moored to the star-seamed bark,
I let the other's illness flow
through well-woven rays of my cloak's sun;
bright stitch of its moon.

Soot and grime smear my staff; venom
splashes my prow; stench swells
from a fang-staved slime.

I leap forward, drum harder; dance
up cloud-steps, mist-rungs; higher,
air thinning, brightening;
my craft the drum's skin;
the skin of my hand,
drum skin.

My spirits twist loose
from medallions of hawk and owl;
from a mountain-shaped pendant
the width of a dream;
from my cloak's hem.

They take the shape
of cymbals, bells; shimmer
from hollows of my club's spikes;

appear as shells,
as spindrift.

We pry open the feverous mouth; I grasp
a sharp-toothed cord
coiling the suffer's tongue; rip it loose,
freeing the soul.

Soul in hand, I climb
a cloud-studded ladder; my spirits return
to root and leaf.

I wake as I restore soul to body:
her eyes open; cured.

The blood that brimmed a pine-scented bowl
has dried. The mare's heart, praised
for breadth and weight, beats
within my sky-blue drum.

The Shaman Comforts the Fledgling's Soul

I ascended above blood-spattered stone,
circling through root and star
until I reached the narrow crag;
found the fledgling's soul.

Strands of light uncoiled from my down.

I grasped them in my beak and built a nest
no claw could reach.

The fledgling's soul answered my full-throated call,
as I placed it in the nest.

Sky-colored bark shimmered beneath my talons
as the tiny soul's wings healed,
taking the bark's color.

As its strength grew, so did the reach of its dream:

It entered a seed
another's beak had cracked open
in the forest beneath us.

An egg would soon be set
within string and twig-weave.

I promised to keep close by that fledgling's
well-dream-nurtured soul
until its cloud-roads opened.

The Shaman's Journey

I was bound to a tree as the singing began.

Dancers used claw-tipped stakes
to jab the soil; I shook loose
from my skin; rose
through a moon-shaped medallion
hung from a pine.

Within a rainbow's hollow bones,
my jade-adorned feathers
began to murmur. I cut free
a beakful of sky: its shadow
took the shape of a door.

I forced it ajar; pressed into the dark.

My wings held steady: gravity stiffened;
lungs ached; soot and ash
clung to my crest.

At a defile: mildewed diaries;
muddied statues, worn featureless; heaps
of rusted dials.

After seven days, a threshold
etched with names; strewn with torn collars,
children's rattles.

Beings less substantial than their hearth's flame
beckoned me: but I flew on,
knowing I could never depart

if I echoed their dread; was scorched
by their tears.

Finally, cowering
within spines of a split-open shell,
I found the soul
I'd come to retrieve.

Placing it in my pouch,
I turned back: Once returned to its body
the blisters would heal.

Below, bent coins twisted from the grit; cries rose
from shards of once-loved words.

I could not pause; though my wings
seemed to bend
from the sound's weight.

After nine days: a cloud-ringed gate
shouldered by stars.

I bellowed my song: awed the gatekeeper;
descending, sea spray
cooled my wings.

I thrust the other's soul into the bedridden body; he rose.

When I awoke, a cup
of pine-scented water
was offered, and I began
to tell this tale.

The Shaman Speaks with the Mother of the Sea Beasts

I rose on wings the weight of a wind-borne seed;
width of a sunrise.

All my spirits within me: fixed to sinew; coiling talon.

I dove the emptied fathoms; followed
a track of smashed bones;
pressed through the jet-black gate.

The guardian moved aside:
cowered by my spirits' masks; the majesty
of my blood-red stride.

Unscathed, I descended
a sea valley's narrow tongue, my plumage
glowing, sparking.

I soon scaled a coral wall
the Mother of the Sea Beasts
had raised in anger
to shelter her children.

I was sure I could soothe her; straighten
her matted hair.

She, in rags, pressed fin to stone; gouged her scales.

Fangs lunged for my crest as I grasp a comb: My spirits
held firm, bellowed to her sentries
that I was flesh and blood
beneath the pulse
of my ever-changing shape.
I brushed out broken shells; spoke of hunger,
illness, regret.

She answered through my spirits' chants,
telling of her children's wasted lives:
humans who eat without taste,
act without sacrifice,
take without need.
I fashioned a harp from fallen quills:
played; polished the stones
ringing her.

The waters began to clear.

I swept sea mountains' peaks, smoothed
churned sand, placed seed after seed
in the sea's furrows.

So many to feed.

Finally, she set free
all the creatures she'd hidden.

My spirits woke me
as water poured from my mouth;
the chanting ceased.

I had lain on burning coals,
as if on a patch
of damp sand.

I rose, said to those who circled:
I have something to say
about greed.

The Shaman and the Goddess

Spirits burst from the skin of my drum;
nuzzled dream-pulsing stones
illuminating my keel; neighing,
ate the grain I offered.

Harnessed to my bow's beak,
they drew me past the House of Night:
through black water's claw-strew tides,
beyond an undertow's bloodied mouth;
into the calm of star-cloak and mist.

Once moored to the sky's navel,
I watched swirls of dark and light converge; stood
on the four-cornered peak.

The gate I'd sought opened
as I spoke my true name,
first uttered by fire-souls
who keep my drum's skin taut.

I entered the House of Day as the Goddess descended.

"Remember," she said, "what is
is all that can be, regardless of breadth
or gleam; breath or rot.

"What is may seem less so, whether whole,
torn, culled; poorly carved
or half-thought-out.

"*What is not is unknowable*. Engrave this
on your craft's mast; *nothing else is* on your prow.
no mortal can then dissuade you
when you return."

With this, the gate reopened; I descended,
setting aside my feather-bright mask.

The Shaman Meets with the First of the Dead

I preened my wings with a scented shell;
nine days and nights, clutched
a summit's razor-sharp peak; whispered
my spirits' chants; watched souls
billow from fissure and crag.

When a white-hot coal fell from my crest,
wind filled my drum's sails. Its prow rose,
breaking free from the precipice.

My beak gleamed
as I sped through moonlit narrows,
toward the darkened place.

When my keel's timber cried, "The way is open,"
I entered the furthest port.

Even my spirits fell back
as I passed through a blood-filled gut;
through ashes and rot.

Claws engraved on my hull took hold;
steadied me.

Beyond a bridge the width of a final word,
I found what others only imagine:
the shadowless one
who was, yet is.

The being appeared at a pillar's top; below,
vastness without equal.

I offered a dream
dreamt by a spirit my ancestors had tamed.

The being grew brighter, churning
from form to form; some familiar, some grotesque.

When it became a drum's skin, I drew it
across my talons,
began to beat in a cadence
it seemed I'd always known; sing
in languages
I'd never spoken.

The stronger my voice, the more I changed form: reeled
through soul after soul,
until my being
became that one at the pillar's top,
sparks shooting
from all I sensed.

The Shaman and the Oracle

The deads' outstretched hands greeted me
as I ascended the five-storied shrine.

Once through a sky-trough's bloodied knives,
I lazed at the tiller of my drum; lowered a mask
shaped from star-bright pebbles.

Below, as the chosen ones chanted
by a fire where my body lie, I moored
to a cloud's loam-scented rib.

The soul of a priestess sat upon a tripod before me, singing:
veil lowered; laurels in hand; incense rising
from a rainbow's sigh.

I lolled as my drum's hull swayed to her rhymes –
but her temple's columns began to fall!

One of the spirits who serve me
grasped her soul's hem
before it frayed; another
led her soul to its nest.

My work could begin.

I shaped a new tripod
from a shell's lungs, columns
from the colors of my keel; cut a hole in the sky
the width of her veil,
so her songs could still be dreamed.

The Shaman Visits the House of Dust

Light I'd gathered from whitecap and cloud,
kept my craft
from the gatekeeper's sight.

I set my beak beneath the snake-shaped gunwales,
drum still; inched prow nearer the threshold
as another crossed.

That being drew its last breath
as I swerved past the scribe:
that other's name struck
from a tablet's ever-soft clay.

Silent, mote-sized, I eased my craft above souls
shredding their final dreams; circled
miles-long tables
where the breathless
chewed lumps of dirt, muddied water
spilling from their cups.

Words spoken of the dead in jest
hung from their mouths.

One tried in vain to restore its charred portrait.

The scale of its cries stirred my drum's skin:
a patch of keel showed. But it failed
to notice; to toss its
barbed net.

Breath held, I forced my prow further down;
crossed beneath the final bridge.
Mooring, I found the flower-scented chamber:
The eldest one hovered
above a nine-limbed tree.

Gifts were offered; mercy given
when deserved. A line of souls
bowed in turn, waited.

I had come to seek a cure; put beak
to drum.

The eldest one gestured.

I presented a blade
hammered from lightning bolt shards; an arrow
shaped from white-hot coals
cooled on my tongue.

The eldest one offered me a cedar chest.

As I gazed at the lid it seemed
I could see nothing else:

even through my thousand-fold hawk's eyes;
though perched at a height
greater than I had ever flown.

Even with world-spanning wings
fully opened,
it dwarfed my plumes.

I couldn't hear my drum; taste,
though my barbed snake's tongue
lapped the darkness.
It took the will of all my spirits to lift the lid.

As I began to decipher
lines cut across its lapis lazuli,
my talons lost hold: I woke

to chanting; dancers circling
the pit where I lie.

I could still see its sky-blue carvings
as I rose to sing:
a map, a way through;
a measure of mercy
for those who must die.

The Shaman Rises From the Waters of Death

As keel was freed from sand and stone,
my beak twisted free
from a stilled face.

None could see this; all believed.

When the craft cradling me
reached the horizon, those on shore
knew I'd rise; wing
from bark to starry branch.

I pushed my prow beneath whitecaps
as the moon
began its chant.

My talons grasped rungs of light; what had bound me
shook loose.

I watched as my next body
began to pulse
from sea to womb.

ACKNOWLEDMENTS

A number of these poems were inspired by the work of Mircea Eliade: *Shamanism, Archaic Techniques of Ecstasy,* Princeton University Press, 2004. His unsurpassed work on shamanism presented this poet with numerous revelatory examples of a shaman's transcendental understanding of the sacred.

Grateful acknowledgment is made to the editors of the following publications in which many of these poems originally appeared: *Crossing the River: An Anthology in Honor of Sacred Journeys, Eternal Haunted Summer, Fickle Muses, Moon Magazine, Mythic Circle, Paper Cuts,* and *Silver Birch Press.*

ABOUT THE AUTHOR

Joseph Murphy has been published in a wide range of print and online journals, including *The Ann Arbor Review*, *Northwind* and *The Sugar House Review*. He is the author of three previous poetry collections, *Shoreline of the Heart, Having Lived* and *Crafting Wings*. Murphy is also a member of the Colorado Authors' League and for eight years (2010–18) was poetry editor for an online literary publication, *Halfway Down the Stairs*.

Visit his website to learn more about his poetry and read excerpts from each collection:

www.josephmurphypoet.com

Middle Creek Publishing Titles

Span   David Anthony Martin

Deepening the Map   David Anthony Martin

Phases   Erika Moss Gordon

Cirque & Sky   Kathleen Willard

Messiah Complex and Other Stories   Michael Olin-Hitt

Lessons from Fighting The Black Snake at Standing Rock   Nick Jaina and Leslie Orihel

Wild Be   One Leaf

Bijoux   David A. Martin

Sawhorse   Tony Burfield

Almost Everything, Almost Nothing   KB Ballentine

Kimono Mountain   Mike Parker

p a l e o s   Hoag Holmgren

I   Bengt O Björklund

Across the Light   Bruce Owens

Faces of Fishing Creek   Kyle Laws

No Better Place: A New Zen Primer   Hoag Holmgren

Secondary Cicatrices   Lynne Goldsmith

A Daughter's Aubade   Mara Adamitz Scrupe

Unraveling The Endless Knot   Sandra Noel

The Shaman Speaks   Joe Murphy

A Wild Silence   John Noland

Sphinx   Andrea Dejean

The Gorund Nest   David Anthony Martin

ABOUT MIDDLE CREEK PUBLISHING

MIDDLE CREEK PUBLISHING believes that responding to the world through art & literature — and sharing that response — is a vital part of being an artist.

MIDDLE CREEK PUBLISHING is a company seeking to make the world a better place through both the means and ends of publishing. We are publishers of quality literature in any genre from authors and artists, both seasoned and as-yet undervalued, with a great interest in works which may be considered to be, illuminate or embody any aspect of contemplative Human Ecology, defined as the relationship between humans and their natural, social, and built environments.

MIDDLE CREEK's particular interest in Human Ecology, is meant to clarify an aspect of the quality in the works we will consider for publication, and is meant as a guide to those considering submitting work to us. Our interest is in publishing works illuminating the Human experience through words, story or other content that connects us to each other, our environment, our history and our potential deeply and more consciously.

www.ingramcontent.com/pod-product-compliance
Lightning Source LLC
Chambersburg PA
CBHW022126090426
42743CB00008B/1022